OBJECTION!

Have You Got What It Takes to Be a Lawyer?

by Lisa Thompson

Compass Point Books ✦ Minneapolis, Minnesota

First American edition published in 2009 by
Compass Point Books
151 Good Counsel Drive
P.O. Box 669
Mankato, MN 56002-0669

Editor: Marissa Bolte
Designer: Ashlee Suker
Art Director: LuAnn Ascheman-Adams
Creative Director: Joe Ewest
Editorial Director: Nick Healy
Managing Editor: Catherine Neitge
Content Adviser: Leigh-Wai Doo, A.B. Columbia, J.D. Harvard Law School;
        former assistant director of legal education in Hawaii;
        founding assistant dean of the University of Hawaii School of Law,
        Honolulu, Hawaii

Editor's note: To best explain careers to readers, the author has created composite characters based on extensive interviews and research. This book is designed to familiarize a young reader thinking of a career in law in the United States. By necessity a generalized, simplified explanation has been given. There are in many instances, exceptions, or methods that may, in specific circumstances, be different from presented.

This book was manufactured with paper containing at least 10 percent post-consumer waste.

Library of Congress Cataloging-in-Publication Data
Thompson, Lisa, 1969–
  Objection! : have you got what it takes to be a lawyer? / by Lisa Thompson.—
1st American ed.
    p. cm.—(On the job)
  Includes index.
  ISBN 978-0-7565-4219-1 (library binding)
  1. Law—Vocational guidance—United States—Juvenile literature.
I. Title. II. Series.
  KF297.T456 2010
  340.023'73—dc22   2009009876

Visit Compass Point Books on the Internet at *www.compasspointbooks.com*
or e-mail your request to *custserv@compasspointbooks.com*

Table of Contents

Monday Morning— It All Begins

8:30 A.M.—I arrive at my office and check my e-mail. Several clients have contacted me about their cases. One of them was seriously injured in an automobile accident, and I need to organize a complaint to file in civil court for him. He is now recovering in the hospital, and I've arranged to meet with him this afternoon.

9 A.M.—I receive a call from a woman, Ann Watson, who needs legal advice. Her father has died and she needs my help in sorting out his will. I make an appointment to meet with her tomorrow.

Hit-and-run accidents can be serious.

9:30 A.M.—I'm still working on the auto accident complaint when my next appointment arrives. He's a young construction worker who was injured at work. I take notes as he explains his story. He has an excellent case for workers' compensation because of unsafe work practices.

As a lawyer, I meet people from all walks of life. Sadly, many of them are in stressful situations, such as a divorce, an injury, an unfair dismissal from work, a criminal charge, an arrest, or a drunken driving offense. Being a lawyer can be both challenging and rewarding.

Injuries can happen when there are poor health and safety standards in the workplace.

11 A.M.—My colleague, Annabel Martin, calls me from the courthouse. She spends most of her time appearing there, and she's currently representing our client who was injured in a car accident. We believe the other driver was at fault for reckless driving.

Annabel tells me the defendant's lawyer has not shown up for his pretrial court appearance today.

For our client's sake, we want the trial to go ahead as quickly as possible. I make my way over to the courthouse to plead our case for the judge to set a date for the trial to proceed, and luckily she agrees with us—the trial date is set.

All this has happened, and it's only lunchtime!

What's in a word

A lawyer is a person who has a law degree and a license to practice law. The word *lawyer* means different things in different countries. In England and other commonwealth countries, such as Canada and Australia, lawyers can mean both solicitors and barristers. Solicitors offer legal counsel outside of court, and barristers argue in court. In the United States, lawyers are also called attorneys and perform the duties of both solicitors and barristers.

Strong research skills are important.

Traits needed to be a good lawyer:

- ability to identify the core issue, analyze, and solve complex problems
- capacity to think through large amounts of written information
- critical thinking skills
- good communication skills
- ability to handle confidential information privately
- organizational and planning skills
- professional attitude
- strong reading and research skills
- ability to work in a professional and ethical manner
- ability to work both independently and in a team
- capacity to work in a practical and orderly manner

How I Became a Lawyer

I grew up in a small, rural town, and like a lot of kids who grow up in the country, I couldn't wait to visit the city after I finished high school. After graduation I started college, where I studied business and political science.

I spent my prelaw internship working for the district attorney's office. My main responsibilities were collecting information on the cases, sorting evidence, contacting witnesses, and performing clerical work, such as making copies or delivering documents. My free hours were spent in courtrooms, watching the cases.

Learn from those in the business—they have great tips.

After I finished my undergraduate degree and took the Law School Admission Test, it was time to start law school.

The LSAT

The Law School Admission Test, also known as the LSAT, is required for entry into law school. Given four times a year, it is a half-day test consisting of multiple-choice tests broken up into sections.

Passing the bar

The Multistate Bar Examination, also known as the bar exam or the MBE, is required for law school graduates who wish to practice law and enter the job market after law school. It is usually a two-day test that lasts six hours each day. There are 200 multiple-choice questions that cover all aspects of law. There is also an essay section. If a lawyer wants to practice in a particular state, he or she must take that state's bar exam, even if he or she has already passed the exam in another state.

Review courses are available for those who want help preparing for the exam.

I passed the bar exam and was ready to practice law. After three years of hard work, I decided to leave the city and go back to the country. That's where I started working for a small firm in a rural town. Most of my friends thought I was crazy—a small-town practice instead of a big-city firm?

Most of the cases we work on deal with criminal law, family law, and workers' compensation claims. Regardless of whether you work in the country or the city, people should have access to excellent legal representation.

Famous Law Schools

Harvard University, Cambridge, Massachusetts
Established in 1636, Harvard University is the oldest institution of higher learning in the United States. The school employs around 1,900 faculty members and has 20,000 students. Seventy-five Nobel Prize winners have been affiliated with the university. Its law school, which opened in 1817, is one of America's oldest. Every year more than 7,000 applicants fight for one of the 500 spots in the first-year law program.

Harvard Law School alumni include Barack Obama, Michelle Obama, Elizabeth Dole, and Janet Reno.

The Ivy League

The term *Ivy League* is used to refer to academic excellence. Eight private schools of higher learning are a part of the Ivy League: Brown University, Columbia University, Cornell University, Dartmouth College, Harvard University, Princeton University, the University of Pennsylvania, and Yale University.

Yale University, New Haven, Connecticut

Since its founding in 1701, Yale University has educated three presidents of the United States, 45 Cabinet members, and more than 500 members of Congress. In addition, two more presidents have graduated from its law school. The Yale Law School is very selective and accepts about 200 new students a year from the 3,000 who apply.

Yale Law School alumni include Hillary Rodham Clinton and two former presidents, Bill Clinton and Gerald Ford.

Stanford University, Palo Alto, California

Stanford University was founded in 1876. Its legal studies department was created in 1893 when former president Benjamin Harrison became the school's first professor of law. Every year from 4,000 to 5,000 candidates apply for the school's available 170 seats in the law program. The school offers nearly 200 courses relating to law.

Stanford Law School alumni include Herbert Hoover, Sandra Day O'Connor, and William Rehnquist.

Who's Who in the Courtroom

Many people play roles in the courtroom during criminal trials.

Bailiff—*court officer who keeps order in court and takes care of both the jury and prisoners while at court*

Court reporter—*types a transcript of everything that is said in the case*

Witness—*presents evidence to the court*

Clerk

Defendant—*the person accused of a crime*

Probation officer

Defense counsel—*represents the defendant*

Civil differences

In civil trials, the defendant is the person or organization that the complaint is against. The plaintiff is the person who initiated the trial by making the complaint against the defendant.

Twelve people = a jury

A jury consists of 12 members of the community who are randomly selected for each case. The judge, and in some cases the lawyers on both sides, decide if members should serve on the jury. If a potential member is found to have any personal interest in the case or could cause an impartial verdict, he or she may not be selected.

A jury decides if an accused person is guilty. Sometimes a jury's decision of guilt or innocence must be unanimous. For other cases, only most of the jurors need to agree.

Judge—*decides the outcomes of court cases*

Law clerk—*assists the judge with research regarding the case*

Prosecuting attorneys— *make a case against the defendant*

Audience

Jury—*hears the evidence and decides the facts, determining whether the accused is guilty of a crime.*

13

Fields of Law

Corporate law

The lawyers make sure agreements, policies, and processes are legal and that companies don't break the law.

Employment and workplace law

Employment lawyers advise employees and employers about legal issues in the workplace, such as hiring and dismissals and health and safety standards. Law firms usually advise either employers or employees, but not both.

Family law

Family lawyers handle cases having to do with child custody, divorce, and property settlements.

It's our job to make sure contracts are legal.

Employers need to look after their employees.

Entertainment law

As an entertainment lawyer, my friend Renee advises and represents people who work in the entertainment industry. This includes people who work in television, sports, music, film, theater, print, and media advertising. Cases may involve copyright issues (who has the right to use or distribute creative works, such as songs or movies), contracts, and personality rights.

Immigration law

Every country has different immigration laws. Immigration lawyers, like my friend Cris, advise people who want to become citizens of a country, or want to live and work temporarily in a new country.

Musicians copyright their music.

Photographers may own the rights to their photos. That means anyone who wishes to use these photos has to buy them from the photographer.

15

Criminal law

Criminal lawyers defend people who are accused of breaking the law. As a criminal lawyer, my friend Tyson handles cases ranging from murder and Internet fraud to drunken driving.

Manuscripts and screenplays are protected under copyright law.

SCREENPLAY

DA VINCI 6d

SANDA ISLAND

16

Intellectual property law

Intellectual property lawyers deal with issues concerning patents, industrial designs, fine art works, and copyright of written works, films, and images.

One of my colleagues, Jo, works as a patent lawyer. Patent law is one type of intellectual property law. It protects people who invent products from people who may use the products without approval.

Copyright law is another type of intellectual property law. It protects people who might have their written works, music, artwork, or other creations copied illegally.

Real estate law

Real estate lawyers specialize in issues having to do with land and property, such as mortgages, leases, homes for sale, and land ownership.

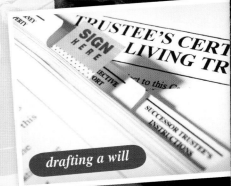

Trusts, estates, and wills

In many countries, lawyers are the only ones who can legally create wills, trusts, and other documents related to a person's property after his or her death. In the United States, people can write their own wills. There are even Internet sites that can help you write a will. But it's still good to have a lawyer's advice.

drafting a will

PUN FUN The short fortune teller who escaped from prison was a small medium at large.

Personal injury law

Personal injury lawyers work on cases in which someone has been injured because of another person or business' negligence, such as automobile accidents or slips and falls.

Lawyerspeak

Lawyers often sound as though they are speaking a foreign language, so it's important to make sure our clients understand what we're talking about.

Acquit—when a defendant is found not guilty in a criminal trial

Affidavit—written statement of facts, signed in front of an official; the person signing the legal document states that the contents are true, to the best of his or her knowledge

Alibi—statement of being somewhere else when a crime was committed

Appeal—request for a superior court to review and perhaps change the outcome of a previously decided case

Bail—money or property given to the court to allow the defendant's release from jail until the court date

Brief—written document submitted by lawyers to the court to support their argument; it includes information about the case, identifies the issues, and cites relevant laws and court decisions; it also explains how the laws relate to the facts

Civil law—law relating to private rights and the codes of law in a society; the plaintiff can be anyone, including governments, businesses, and individuals; a verdict does not have to be unanimous—both the plaintiff and the defendant can appeal the decision; penalties can only be monetary

Criminal law—law relating to criminal activity; the plaintiff is always the state or federal government; the jury decision in a criminal trial must be unanimous; the defendant is found guilty or not guilty, and can appeal the decision; punishments include jail or prison time, fines, and, in some states, executions

Cross-examination—questioning a witness about details involving the case by the lawyer on the opposing side

Deposition—testimony of a witness, taken before the trial by lawyers in the case; this is a way for lawyers to discover evidence ahead of time

Evidence—facts about the case, such as physical evidence, like fingerprints, or information about the defendant that lawyers use in court

Habeas corpus—legal document commanding that a person be brought before a judge; it is a way to require that a judge look into the legality of holding someone in prison

Injunction—an order prohibiting a certain action from being carried out by a person or group

Manslaughter—causing an accidental death

Objection—an attorney's complaint to the judge about another attorney's action in court; objections can be overruled (not allowed) or sustained

Why Latin?

Although Latin is rarely spoken anymore, many Latin words are used in law and medicine. In fact, 60 percent of the words in the English language derive from Latin.

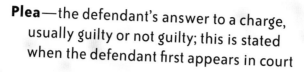

Plea—the defendant's answer to a charge, usually guilty or not guilty; this is stated when the defendant first appears in court

Pro bono—providing a service free of charge

Quid pro quo—the equal exchange of goods or services

Subpoena—court order requiring a witness to appear in court to give evidence

Voir dire—process by which lawyers choose or reject prospective jurors

At some time, almost everyone needs a lawyer.

The Law Through Time

There has never been a society that existed without some form of law.

399 B.C.
Greek philosopher Socrates is accused of refusing to accept Athenian gods and of corrupting young people by spreading his beliefs. He is found guilty and sentenced to death.

c. 30 A.D.
Jesus is accused of blasphemy and condemned to death.

1633
Galileo Galilei is put on trial for heresy against the Catholic Church. He is found guilty. His punishment includes signing a public statement admitting that his belief in a sun-centered solar system was wrong; the statement is then read at every Italian university. Copies of his book are burned, and Galileo is imprisoned in his home until he dies in 1642.

1692
Four young girls in Salem, Massachusetts, suffer from a mysterious illness. The illness is blamed on witchcraft, beginning the Salem Witch Trials. Nineteen people are sent to trial, accused of being witches, and sentenced to death; dozens more are imprisoned.

1862

After fighting ended between American settlers and the Dakota Sioux, 303 Dakota are found guilty of crimes against Americans and sentenced to death. President Abraham Lincoln spares 265 of the prisoners, but the remaining 38 are executed by hanging in Mankato, Minnesota. This event, which ended the Dakota Conflict, is the largest mass execution in American history.

1911

A fire at the Triangle Shirtwaist Factory in New York City kills 146 workers, mostly girls, who are unable to escape the building. The owners of the company, Max Blanck and Isaac Harris, are taken to court on charges of manslaughter.

1925

A Tennessee bill called the Butler Act declares that it is unlawful for teachers in public schools to deny the story of creationism from the Bible and to teach any theories involving evolution. Schoolteacher John Scopes is taken to trial for openly teaching the theory to his class. Scopes is found guilty and fined. The anti-evolution laws are not lifted until the 1960s.

1932

The baby of famous airman Charles Lindbergh is kidnapped from his nursery. After the $50,000 ransom is paid, the baby's body is found. Two years later, new evidence indicates carpenter Bruno Hauptmann could be the kidnapper. Hauptmann is accused of the crime and is sent to trial. He is found guilty and sentenced to death.

1954

Lawyer Thurgood Marshall presents the case *Brown v. Board of Education* to the United States Supreme Court. The Supreme Court unanimously decides that segregation in the schools is illegal and that separate educational facilities are not equal. Thirteen years later, Marshall is named the first African-American Supreme Court justice by President Lyndon B. Johnson.

1970

Charles Manson is charged with seven counts of murder and one count of conspiracy. He is found guilty and originally given the death penalty. The sentence is reduced to life in prison in 1972 when California abolishes the death penalty. A separate trial in 1971 finds him guilty of two more murders, and he is given another life sentence.

1995

Former NFL star O.J. Simpson is accused of murdering his former wife, Nicole Brown Simpson, and her friend Ron Goldman. After an eight-month trial, the longest in California history, Simpson is found not guilty. In 1997 a civil court finds him liable for the deaths and orders Simpson to pay the Brown and Goldman families $33.5 million. In 2008 he was sentenced to nine years in prison for an attempted robbery.

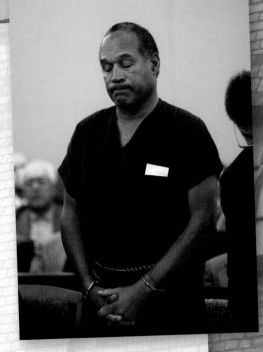

1998

Sixteen bombs disguised as packages are discovered between 1978 and 1995, killing three people and injuring 23 more. The search for the bomber becomes one of the most expensive investigations in FBI history. Ted Kaczynski, also known as the Unabomber, is found and arrested in 1996. Two years later, he is found guilty and sentenced to life in prison without parole.

2006

Former Iraqi leader Saddam Hussein is found guilty of crimes against humanity and executed. He had been captured in 2003 after the U.S. and several allies invaded Iraq.

The Two Courts

There are two major branches of the court system: state and federal.

The state systems vary from state to state. Most trials held in the United States take place at state court. Those courts are organized as follows:

- Inferior court (including municipal, divorce, juvenile, small-claims, police, and traffic court)—handles minor civil and criminal cases

- Superior court (sometimes known as state district court or circuit court)—hears appeals from inferior courts, major civil suits, and serious criminal cases; most jury trials are held in superior court

- Appellate court (sometimes called the state court of appeals or state supreme court)—hears appeals from lower state courts

Millions and millions

State courts in the United States handle more cases than federal courts. About 30 million cases are filed in state courts each year. About 1 million cases are filed in federal courts each year.

A job for life

The president of the United States of America appoints justices to the U.S. Supreme Court. Supreme Court justices hold their position for life.

PUN FUN

A prisoner's favorite punctuation mark is the period. It marks the end of a sentence.

Like the state system, the federal system is divided into three levels.

- Federal district courts—handle violations of the Constitution and other federal laws, cases involving a state or the federal government, maritime disputes, and cases involving foreign citizens or governments

- Courts of appeals—13 judicial circuits; hear appeals from the federal district courts and handle cases involving federal agencies

- Supreme Court—hears appeals from the courts of appeals and handles cases involving high-level diplomats or cases between states

Children in the Courtroom

In most countries, children who are charged with committing a crime are not tried in court as adults. The United States does not have one juvenile justice system—instead, each state and the District of Columbia sets its own procedures for handling juveniles.

Juvenile court deals with matters involving children under the ages of 15, 16, or 17 (depending on the state).

- Delinquency cases include those in which a law is broken by a minor. These laws can range from breaking curfew to committing murder.

Juvenile cases are often very stressful for parents.

- Child protection cases are filed when a child's parents are accused of putting the child's health or welfare at risk. Some examples include physical or substance abuse and custody cases.

Most delinquency cases are private; however, if the crime is serious enough and the defendant is older than 16, the proceedings can be made public. Most child protection cases are open to the public.

PUN FUN If a lawyer can be disbarred, can a model be deposed or a singer be denoted?

Young adults

If the crime is severe enough, a child can be tried as an adult. In 1999 an 11-year-old Michigan boy was tried for and found guilty of murder as an adult.

Trials can be confusing—we need to make sure our clients know what's going on!

Children worldwide

Since World War II, countries have made significant progress in creating laws to protect:

- children's health
- children's right to education
- children from abuse and exploitation
- children's rights in the legal system

For some, there are serious consequences.

Breaking the Law

Although most trials in movies and on TV focus on murder cases, there are many other ways to break the law.

- **arson**—deliberate burning of a structure or area
- **assault**—act that threatens physical harm to another person
- **conspiracy**—planning to commit a crime with others

"Will the witness please identify who they saw commit the crime?"

- **credit card fraud**—unlawful use of a credit card; this includes the theft, use, sale, or forgery of credit cards; the use of a credit card with the knowledge that the card has been revoked or expired, or does not have enough available credit to pay for the charged items; and the buying of items knowing that the credit card is being used illegally

- **DUI/DWI**—driving while under the influence of alcohol or drugs

- **embezzlement**—theft of money or property by someone entrusted to look after the assets

- **first-degree murder**—planned and intentional killing of another person

- **manslaughter**—falls under two categories; voluntary refers to the intentional but unplanned killing of someone; involuntary refers to the unintentional killing of someone

- **perjury**—lying after taking an oath to tell the truth

- **second-degree murder**—unlawful killing of a person without intent

Powers of arrest

If police officers reasonably suspect that a person has committed, or is about to commit, a crime, they can arrest that person. However, police officers should use arrest as a last resort. Resisting arrest is a serious offense and is punishable by fines, probation, or even jail time.

Preparing a Criminal Case

The fist step is to draw up a case plan. The case plan includes a list of all the relevant documents, statements, and names of witnesses. My team and I will need these to help us build our case.

These documents may include:

- any relevant tests, including blood or DNA tests
- statements from specialists, such as doctors
- list of evidence from the crime scene
- police statements
- client statements
- witness statements

Taped conversations may be admitted as evidence.

evidence from a crime scene

EVIDENCE

State Police
Fingerprint Record

Right Hand

Thumb | Index Finger | Middle Finger | Ring Finger | Pinky Finger

Left Hand

Index Finger | Thumb

Evidence

If the defendant appearing in court pleads not guilty, then it's time to prepare for the trial. We need to make a file that contains all the written statements and exhibits that the prosecution will use to argue their case against the defendant. This may include things the defendant has said.

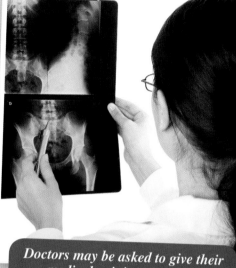

Doctors may be asked to give their medical opinions in court.

Exhibits are pieces of physical evidence police collect from a crime scene, such as clothing, footprints, or blood. Sometimes experts examine the crime scene or evidence and give their expert opinion on these things in court. The defendant's lawyer analyzes the evidence to build a case that will prove his or her client's innocence.

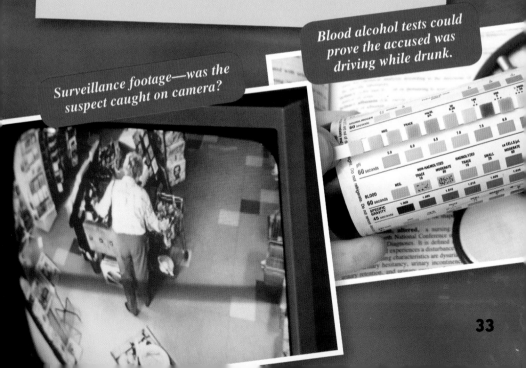

Blood alcohol tests could prove the accused was driving while drunk.

Surveillance footage—was the suspect caught on camera?

33

Updates on My Cases

Auto accident—Witness statements

My co-counsel Sarah Charleston looks over our evidence file to prepare for her court appearance. The brief contains statements from three witnesses. The witnesses are a man who owns a store across from the accident scene, an elderly lady who was walking her dog, and a young boy who was playing with a ball nearby.

The statements describe what these three people saw—the color of the car that hit my client, what the driver looked like, what time the accident occurred, and whether they remember the car's license plate number. She needs to make sure her witnesses are calm and completely prepared before the defense lawyer cross-examines them. The defense will try to prove that her witnesses are unreliable.

Watch out!

Witnesses are not allowed to discuss a case with other witnesses involved in the same case. This prevents any confusion between witnesses' testimonies and avoids any suspicion that they made up the evidence together.

34

Construction worker case

My client and I meet with his former employer's workers' compensation insurance adjuster and lawyer. We ask for a certain amount of money in compensation for my client's injuries. They agree to pay, so this case is closed.

It can take many meetings before both parties agree.

The will and estate case

While meeting with Ann Watson, she says that her family has been arguing over how to divide her father's property. Some family members claim that they aren't getting a fair share.

It's time to reassess the father's property and the conditions of the will, and to meet with Mrs. Watson's family. It gets complicated when families disagree, but I always try to resolve things as best I can.

At the Movies

There are many popular films about lawyers, their work, and what happens in the courtroom. Some are humorous, while others deal with realistic characters and realistic issues.

12 Angry Men

The movie *12 Angry Men* focuses on a jury as it tries to reach a verdict in a murder case. The jury must decide whether an 18-year-old man is guilty of murder. At first the case appears to be straightforward—the defendant has a weak alibi, a knife was left at the murder scene, and several witnesses saw the young man running away from the scene. Eleven of the jurors immediately vote that the young man is guilty—only Juror Number 8, Mr. Davis, thinks he is not guilty. As the story unfolds, and the jury considers the evidence, their prejudices are exposed.

12 Angry Men

Popcorn

The Firm

In *The Firm*, Tom Cruise plays Mitch McDeere, a young man with a promising future in law. As he is about to sit for his bar exam, a large, successful law firm makes an attractive job offer. But the firm isn't exactly what it appears to be, and Mitch is forced to decide between working for it or bringing it to justice.

To Kill a Mockingbird

Based on Harper Lee's prize-winning book, *To Kill a Mockingbird* tells the story of Atticus Finch, a lawyer who lives in Alabama during the 1930s. Though many townspeople try to persuade him not to, Atticus agrees to defend a young African-American man falsely charged with a serious crime. Scout, Atticus' daughter, narrates the story as an adult as she remembers her childhood.

The Firm

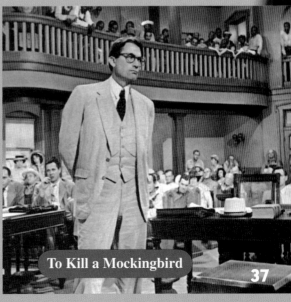

To Kill a Mockingbird

Important Things to Remember

Everyone has a right to be heard in court. If someone is charged with a crime, it doesn't mean that he or she is guilty.

The right to a fair trial—a person has the right to a neutral and detached judge and jury, uninfluenced witnesses, and adequate legal counsel to present his or her case.

Presumption of innocence—a person charged with a criminal offense is presumed not guilty until proven guilty in court.

PUN FUN
A criminal's best asset is his lie-ability.

A lawyer presents his case.

38

Proof beyond reasonable doubt—to convict the accused, the judge or jury has to be satisfied beyond a reasonable doubt that the accused committed that crime. It is the prosecution's job to meet that burden of proof. This means they have to convince the judge or the jury that it's almost certain the accused committed the crime.

The right to remain silent—an accused person has the right to refuse to answer questions. This principle protects the person from making himself or herself appear guilty.

The right of appeal—if the defense or prosecution does not agree with the outcome or procedures in a case, they can appeal.

Rules of evidence—these rules determine what evidence can be admitted in court. One important rule is that witnesses can only give evidence about what they heard, saw, or experienced directly.

When the jury can't decide

Sometimes the jury cannot reach a verdict of guilty or not guilty. In some cases all 12 jurors must reach a unanimous verdict. If the jury can't reach a decision, the accused may have to be retried later with a different jury.

The Judgment Is In

Auto accident case

After three hours, the jury returns with a judgment in my client's favor. The defendant is found negligent because of dangerous driving. My client and I are very pleased with this decision, but I suspect the defendant will appeal the judgment, and we'll soon be back in court.

The will and estate case

I've arranged to meet Ann Watson and her family to sort out the will. I hope we can work something out so that everyone is happy with the result. Ultimately the will's conditions determine how the property and possessions are divided.

The court finds you guilty!

What happens next?

After the jury makes its decision, it's up to the judge to set the penalty in a criminal case. Penalties can include:

- probation
- monetary fines
- community service
- jail or prison time
- treatment for drug or substance abuse
- death (in some states)

What's the difference?

There is a difference between jail and prison. In jail inmates are usually awaiting trial or serving short sentences (less than a year). Jails are usually run by sheriffs or local governments. Prisons are run by state or federal governments. All prison inmates have been tried and convicted. There are about 3,600 jails and nearly 200 prisons in the United States.

Back at the Office

A lot of telephone calls and e-mails await me. I spend the afternoon working on another case and try to respond to as many phone calls as I can.

Being a lawyer is a challenging profession. There is no end to justice, and it is important to keep up the fight. The law protects our rights, our freedom, and our security. As a lawyer, it's my job to ethically and vigorously represent my client's view, and always remember that I am an officer of the court and must behave responsibly.

Opportunities for lawyers

As a lawyer, you could work in these areas:

- **education**—work as a teacher or professor in law schools
- **commercial law**—work with big city law firms and advise corporate business clients
- **individual practice**—work individually and practice in a wide variety of areas, such as estates and family law

- **in-house legal counsel**— work for a company and advise it on how the law affects its business

- **accounting firms**—work in the financial industry, providing legal expertise for financial transactions

- **legal aid or community legal center**—work for government or nongovernment legal organizations helping people who don't have the money to pay for a lawyer

- **politics**—help develop government policies and ways to improve the law and the community, state, or nation

- **judiciary**—work as a judge in a court

- **colleges and universities**—professor and legal researcher in international transactions and disputes between nations and on human rights

- **mediation**—help disputing parties reach a solution to their disagreement

- **negotiator of labor disputes**—negotiate disagreements between employers and employees or labor unions

PUN FUN Old lawyers never die. They just lose their appeal.

Follow These Steps to Become a Lawyer

Step 1

Finish high school, taking courses in English, foreign languages, government, and other subjects in the humanities, which will be useful for a career in the law. Develop skills in reading, writing, speaking, reasoning, and analyzing.

Participate in extracurricular activities such as debate, speech, and drama.

Step 2

Attend college to obtain a bachelor's degree. A prelaw degree is not necessary—degrees in English, communications, political science, and business are equally valued. An internship can help you gain experience as well.

Step 3

Study for and take the LSAT. Apply and get accepted into a law school.

Study for, take, and pass the bar exam. Many law school graduates take a review course before taking the test.

Those wishing to practice law must also be evaluated for good character and fitness. This is designed to help the state bar examiners know whether the applicant has the right character and morals to become a lawyer.

Decide what you want to be and do in life. Decide which part of law you want to specialize in. You're ready to start your new job!

Find Out More

In the Know

- Education at one of the top law schools in the United States, such as Harvard, Yale, and Stanford, isn't cheap. Tuition averages around $40,000 a year.
- About 27 percent of lawyers are self-employed, either running their own firms or working as partners in other firms.
- There are more than 761,000 practicing lawyers in the United States.
- As of 2006, the U.S. Department of Labor estimates that the average wage for a lawyer is $102,470 a year. However, salaries can vary according to what type and amount of work is done, and the location.

Further Reading

Jacobs, Thomas A. *They Broke the Law—You Be the Judge: True Cases of Teen Crime*. Minneapolis: Free Spirit Pub., 2003.

Haugen, Brenda. *Thurgood Marshall: Civil Rights Lawyer and Supreme Court Justice*. Minneapolis: Compass Point Books, 2007.

Haugen, David, and Susan Musser, eds. *Criminal Justice*. Detroit: Greenhaven Press, 2009.

Hunter, David. *Inequities of the Justice System*. Philadelphia: Mason Crest Publishers, 2007.

Internet Sites

FactHound offers a safe, fun way to find Internet sites related to this book. All of the sites on FactHound have been researched by our staff.

Here's all you do:

Visit *www.facthound.com*

FactHound will fetch the best sites for you!

Glossary

bar exam—exam given by a state that lawyers wishing to practice law must pass

copyright—right to publish and sell any artistic work

counsel—lawyer or group of lawyers who represent clients in court

custody—legal right to raise a child

defendant—person being accused of a crime

ethics—accepted principles of behavior

fraud—form of deception done for personal or monetary gain

jury—ordinary people whose job is to decide the facts and verdict in a court case

law firm—business formed by a group of lawyers with the intent to practice law

negligence—failure to provide proper care to a person or object

parole—limited freedom granted to prisoners in exchange for good behavior

perjury—knowingly lying while under oath

plaintiff—person who initiates a trial by complaining against the defendant in a civil matter

probation—suspension of a convicted person's sentence; usually the person is supervised

segregation—practice of separating people of different races

testimony—statements in a legal case that are used for evidence

U.S. Supreme Court—highest judicial body in the United States

verdict—decision of a jury

Index

Look for More Books in This Series:

Art in Action: Have You Got What It Takes to Be an Animator?

Battling Blazes: Have You Got What It Takes to Be a Firefighter?

Behind Every Step: Have You Got What It Takes to Be a Choreographer?

Cleared for Takeoff: Have You Got What It Takes to Be an Airline Pilot?

Cover Story: Have You Got What It Takes to Be a Magazine Editor?

Game On: Have You Got What It Takes to Be a Video Game Developer?

Going Live in 3, 2, 1: Have You Got What It Takes to Be a TV Producer?

Hard Hat Area: Have You Got What It Takes to Be a Contractor?

Head of the Class: Have You Got What It Takes to Be an Early Childhood Teacher?